T0195768

IMAGINARY HEARt

THINGS UNSEEN!

MARCIA JEAN TERPSTRA

authorHOUSE®

AuthorHouse™
1663 Liberty Drive
Bloomington, IN 47403
www.authorhouse.com
Phone: 833-262-8899

Published by AuthorHouse 08/11/2020

ISBN: 978-1-7283-6729-3 (sc)
ISBN: 978-1-7283-6728-6 (hc)
ISBN: 978-1-7283-6727-9 (e)

Library of Congress Control Number: 2020913476

Print information available on the last page.

KJV
Scripture taken from The Holy Bible, King James Version. Public Domain

New Living Translation (NLT)
Holy Bible, New Living Translation, copyright © *1996, 2004, 2015 by Tyndale House Foundation. Used by permission of Tyndale House Publishers, Inc., Carol Stream, Illinois 60188. All rights reserved.*

New King James Version (NKJV)
Scripture taken from the New King James Version®. Copyright © *1982 by Thomas Nelson. Used by permission. All rights reserved.*

ABOUT THE BOOK

This book was conceived in me when I became aware that what I did or did not do with my body became more important to others than the heart that lived within me.

I used the word imaginary in its title because it best described my unseen heart. The images in one's mind far outweighed the reality of all the good that was truly in me.

My greater goal for this book though, was to prove through God's Word that there is a salvation in each and every one of us; no matter who we are, no matter what our walk. Each one of us is the "whosoever" that Jesus died for. And that this gift of salvation cannot be stolen nor stripped away from a single soul; no matter what!

These are not my words. This is God's promise.

Just as you are!

Just as I am!

LAMININ

Colossians 1:15-17 NLT

Christ is the visible image of the invisible God. He existed before anything was created and is supreme over all creation; for through Him God created everything in the heavenly realms and on earth. He made all things we can see and all things we can't see - such as thrones, kingdoms, rulers, and authorities in the unseen world. Everything was created through Him and for Him. He existed before anything else, and

HE HOLDS ALL CREATION TOGETHER.

2 Corinthians 4:18 NLT

So we don't look at the troubles we can see now; rather, we fix our gaze on things that cannot be seen. For the things we see now will soon be gone, but

THE THINGS WE CANNOT SEE
WILL LAST FOREVER.

LAMININ

It is the single molecule that holds all of our being together and it is in the shape of

THE CROSS!

I DEDICATE THIS BOOK TO ANY OF
THOSE WHO BELIEVE THAT THEY
ARE LOST AND UNFORGIVEN!

THERE SIMPLY IS NO TRUTH IN IT!

JUST ASK JESUS!

JOHN 3:16 KJV -17 NLT

16– For God so loved the world, that He gave His only begotten Son, that **WHOSOEVER** believeth in Him should not perish, but have everlasting life.

17– God sent His Son into the world not to judge the world, but to save the world through Him.

IMAGINARY HEARt

THE CHAPTERS

DANDELION DAYS

Blessed are those who
are poor in spirit...

I was born with an impurity within me. I call it the thorn in my flesh. I knew there was no escaping it.

Because of it I was trained to believe that I was a leper in a land where nothing was new under the sun except me. Yet I knew there was a salvation in me. And yet I somehow knew the splendor of my own life.

God is love! I am the spark of life that God ignited me to be.

GOD DESIGNED ME TO BE LIKE NO OTHER!

And, were you there when God created me? Were you there when God blew His breath into me?

Just as every single snowflake that falls from the sky, each one has no likeness to any other snowflake other than all are as white as snow. Each flake has its own creative design. So too, me.

God created me yet my life was a life near lost by all the grumblings of this earth.

But the greater victory for me as I grew in my years on this earth was the understanding that nothing can separate me from the love of God!

Romans 8:38-39 NLT states "And I am convinced that nothing can ever separate us from God's love. Neither death nor life, neither angels nor demons, neither our fears for today nor our worries for tomorrow – not even the powers of hell can separate us from God's love.

No power in the sky above or in the earth below – indeed, nothing in all creation will ever be able to separate us from the love of God that is revealed through Christ Jesus our Lord."

As all humanity, I lived, suffered and gained in life. But mostly I was judged by all mankind.

Even in my very early years I felt the prickling of that thistle in my side. That thistle that later grew into my thorn. I never spoke of it to anyone back then but I felt the doom looming over me as I watched the world around me.

What if that day on December 7, 1956 when man said that I would not live but I would die, that I did die? What if this was not ordained by God? What if God ordained that I take my first breath for Him and that He would carry me to my last breath? What if God looked at what He had made and said that it was good? What if God whispered to me at that moment and said "Just as you are."?

Job 33:4 NLT says "For the Spirit of God has made me, and the breath of the Almighty gives me life."

God gave me purpose. God gave me purpose on that one day; that one instant in time.

I almost chuckle at my life, that moment of my first breath, to where I am today. I chuckle because God knew that I was in no way even close to "normal". He knew I was one of the farthest beings from His original creation yet He birthed me anyway. I can't even begin to imagine the depths I had fallen from God's perfect creation even before I was ever born. Something inside me though still knew I was created

4

in the image of God. I would not have made it into this life if I did not somehow know this. I was a sight in God's eye long before He ever gave me breath.

In my youth I knew that I was so very, very different. Way back then I just did not know in what way I was so very different. It was something inside me. No one could see it and I did not understand it. I could not see it.

After all, I had two hands with five fingers on each of them. I had two arms and two legs. I had two feet with five toes on them as well. I had eyes that could see. I had a nose that could smell. I had ears that could hear. To look at me, I looked very normal.

I had a mouth that could taste. I had feeling to my touch. I had my breath. I had a beating heart. My blood flowed freely through me. I had a strong frame. My mind seemed to be working. I seemed normal in every sense of the word. I was more normal than so many others I had seen around me.

I was not poor. I was birthed into this family with a father and a mother. I had brothers and sisters. I always had a roof over my head. There was always food on the table, three times a day even. I always had clothes on my back and shoes on my feet and coats to wear.

My parents held this all together for me and my six other siblings. My parents never divorced. They took us all to church on Sundays; twice even. My parents in all their provision even managed to pay for each one of their children's Christian education.

I was shoe shined to the hilt yet there was no dancing in me.

I seemed blessed beyond so many could hope for or even imagine. I should have been filled with joy.

So, what was different in me? Why in my soul did I feel this internal deep despair and sense of rejection? What were these caverns and caves that haunted my innocent life? That place of so desperately empty?

Then incest came knocking on my door, still in my youth. I somehow survived it. That almost seemed normal to me compared to this other thing. The incest was the sword on my one side. My thorn was on my other side.

So, which came first, my sword or my thorn? To me it was not debatable. They both hurt. They both brought deep shame into my life.

With time and as I watched the world go by, I understood what my thorn was. I was in my late teens when I braved letting my parents know that I was gay. It did not go well at all. And it did not set well with my siblings either.

Just out of the blue one day, my father called me at my workplace and said to me that he and my mom were going to have me institutionalized. They didn't know what else to do.

I was called demon possessed. I was a curse to the Christian culture I was raised in.

At one point I had all my possessions thrown out of a family members house; a house I considered a safe place. I was called demon possessed there too.

I had no where to go except back to my parent's house. While there I planned and laid in wait until I could make my great escape. There was no other choice but to leave. I went to the right place, away!

It's always been said to me that being gay was a choice I made.

I say back to them, do you really believe I would choose such a path of lifelong persecution?

When I had told those I loved that I was gay, I lost everything! I mean everything! I lost everything I ever knew. I was cast out from my family. I was cast out from my friends. I was cast out from my Christian church. I was cast out from community. I was cast out from even God's Kingdom according to them. I suddenly became like trash on the street.

Most crushing though was when I was told that God would never love me; that I was nothing to Him. And I believed them.

I nearly lost my mind through all of this and my heart was torn to shreds. I carried it with me though as I moved on.

I lost their God back there only to begin my journey to find my own God. The God.

Me, my thorn and my tore up heart went on a long walk together, to seek and to find.

As I walked, I discovered that there was never any darkness so black that I could not see the light of God. There would never be any enemy that was strong enough to snatch me out from under God's wing. There would never be any imperfection in me, not even that thorn, that could strip God's love from me.

After all, I AM a child of God!

My heart was on the mend.

What does it mean in God's Kingdom to own a good heart? What does it mean in man's kingdom to never look inside another's heart to learn of it?

I read in God's Word that the only unpardonable sin is to quench the Spirit of God. I began to ponder the enormous magnitude of this. So, all my other sins are forgiven but if I choke out the Spirit of God, in not only my own life but in any other one's life; this is not forgiven.

This became very complex in my thinking and reasoning. Yet in spirit it makes so much sense. It is really about God's law of love. The flow of His Spirit in me and through me. And the flow of His Spirit in others and through others. The law of love applies to each and every one of us.

When should I have been pulling on one's hand rather than tugging at one's heal?

I continued my walk, me and my thorn.

I talked to God and listened for God everywhere I walked no matter where I went, no matter where my feet landed. I learned more about God in all the wrong places than I ever would have in that barren barn back home.

God began to seep into that empty hole within me. He was there in all my wrong relationships. He was there in all my comings and goings; whether I was soaring or sinking. God was there in my crawl and He was there on my mountaintops. God was there in all my testing and trying. God was there!

God was with me when I walked through the fires. He made sure I did not get burned. But rather He ignited a flame in me.

I began to live somewhere between there and here.

I have often asked myself, "Marcia, if you could do your life over, what would you change?" I replied to myself, "I would be normal. I would marry a nice man that would provide for me. We would have 2.5 children and go to church every Sunday; twice even. And we would live happily ever after on this earth." I see now, this was never God's plan for me.

In and through my life God provided a family for me. They were not blood but they sure were kin to my kind. And there were many of us in our clan.

In my early life especially, I died one piece at a time, bit by bit. This new life with my thorn and I, I was given life over and over again.

My thorn became that of many colors, my rainbow thorn. A covenant between God and I.

My mother once told me, "You always had a hunger for God."

Rainbows and Triangles.

Ecclesiastes 6:10 NLT "Everything has already been decided. It was known long ago what each person would be. So, there's no use arguing with God about your destiny."

The Dandelion

A weed that seems to never die. Yet has an evolution all its own.

The most enduring flower ever that eventually blows into all the wind.

In its youth, its green leaves fold up and embraces its yellow bloom through the night.

Then in the morning the green leaves release themselves from that bloom and the yellow bloom blossoms once again.

Day after day for months on end, the yellow bloom blossoms till one day suddenly without notice, the bloom transforms itself into a cloud of feathers.

Then with a gust of the wind, the feathers are tossed through the air seed by seed.

As I watched, I heard.

"Blow in the wind, Marcia!"
"Blow in the wind for Me."

Psalm 139:14 NLT – "Thank You for making me so wonderfully complex! Your workmanship is marvelous – how well I know it."

Isaiah 40:13-15 NLT

13 – Who is able to advise the Spirit of the Lord? Who knows enough to give Him advice or to teach Him?

14 – Has the Lord ever needed anyone's advice? Does He need instruction about what is good? Did someone teach Him what is right or show Him the path of justice?

15 – No, for all the nations of the world are but a drop in the bucket. They are nothing more than dust on the scales. He picks up the whole earth as though it were a grain of sand.

WEEPING WILLOW

Blessed are those
who mourn...

"The Crawl"
Sunday, May 5, 2019.

On Friday April 19th 2019 I adopted a miniature sheep dog. She was 12 years old. Her name is Gabby. I adopted her after the agonizing death of Starr, my most cherished companion for so many reasons. She was like God incarnate. She was the most spirit filled dog that I had ever owned. The loss of her took a big toll on me.

I inquired about Gabby to try to at least fill a small fraction of all that was missing in me since Starr was now gone. I gaged this decision carefully not just for me but for Badger. Starr raised Badger up so to speak. Badger is my joyful noise in the household. He came with a loud voice. Anyway, Badger was very depressed too. The void of Starr was unbearable for both of us.

As any pet owner knows, you can't replace one pet that is gone with another. It wasn't about that. It was simply about bringing new life into the home.

Gabby was raised on a farm where horses were raised in a barn. She was such a tiny thing. It amazed me she wasn't trampled on in that barn. Gabby's original elderly owners had both passed away. The daughter of this couple was left to find homes for all the animals left on that farm. Lucky me, I got Gabby.

Gabby had lived on this farm all her life so coming into a strange home with strange animals was very hard on her. Gabby was also struggling with her sight and hearing.

On Saturday May 4th, Gabby navigated her way to the far corner of my back yard near the shed. There was a small compose pile there behind some evergreen bushes. I hadn't seen Gabby for a while nor was she responding to my calls for her. So, I went out into the yard to see where she might be. I found her asleep on that compose pile. She seemed lost and all alone. I scooped her up and cradled her in my arms and carried her across the property into the safety of home.

On Sunday May 5th I had one of my weekend conversations with my parents. Out of the blue my mother brought up that "You are still a homosexual." Implying that I could never be saved. I thought my head would spin from off my shoulders. I was in a state of shock. After all we had been through and after all we had talked about and after all these years nothing in her heart had changed towards me. To this day I can't even put into words what went through me. I was shivering.

As the early afternoon went on, I thought I was calming down. I had let the dogs out. Once again, Gabby had not returned to the back door. After a little time went by, I went out looking for her. Once again, I found her sleeping on that compose pile by the shed. I reached down to scoop her up. This time I could not get a grip on her. My legs would not support me. I tried several more times to pick Gabby up and with each time my legs became more like noodles. There was no strength in them at all.

I tried for my last time to gather Gabby up only for my legs to collapse from underneath me. I fell with my belly to the ground. I tried using my arms to get up but after repeated tries even they became like noodles. I grabbed at a branch to see if I could pull myself up in that way but not even that worked. My arms were too weak and my legs just wouldn't come out from under me.

With my face to the ground now and on my belly, I began to think how I would ever get across that vast yard and even if I did would I ever be able to stand? There was no other choice but to try.

I tried putting my hands to the earth to grip it in order to drag myself. My arms just would not work. I tried using my feet to dig into the ground to push myself forward. I might have moved three inches. I then just tried wiggling my belly to try to make any forward motion at all. I was getting nowhere. I just laid the side of my face in the dirt wondering how long I would be there and what would happen to Gabby.

After laying there in what seemed an eternity, I heard someone calling my name several times over. I lifted my head and before I could say I needed help my neighbor John and his girlfriend came running through my gate. Without hesitation they scooped me up by my armpits and lifted me to my back door. At that moment I was able to stand on my own two feet once again.

They asked me what happened and I mumbled something about being a homosexual and how I was still being rejected by family.

The crawl with no salvation in sight.

It was nearly impossible growing up gay, and to make it through. The suffering in silence, the public stoning, the sheer loneliness, the isolation, the anguish, the shame and sorrow. And even after we found each other, the gays alike; these things never left any of us.

Then on top of all this, to add those amongst us who were murdered by those outside of us and those of us beaten and left for dead. And those amongst us who took their own lives because of all that was so unbearable.

No. This was not a party. This was painful. We did our best to hide our mourning clothes. But we could never get them off our backs nor out of our hearts.

And yes, we do have hearts!

I have been working on this book for nearly ten years now; waiting and wanting to be sure that all its contents were in right standing with God. And almost equally important was that I would finally be brave enough to tell the truth. The truth of what it was like growing up gay and surviving it.

As I write nearing the end of this book, the whole world is suffering from the COVID-19 pandemic. A foreign ground to all humanity. And as I sit in my little world and how this has affected my life, I strangely began to experience PTS; a post-traumatic stress. A reliving of my past.

I had been here before. A remembrance of grief, of deep sorrow that began to overwhelm me. This was all to familiar to me, like when I lived through the AIDS era. The epidemic of my day, turned pandemic.

In the early phases of the AIDS epidemic, no one, not even the scientist could explain how this disease was transmitted. No one could say for sure whether it was through touch or saliva or blood. No one knew so everyone became afraid or at least until it was titled the "gay disease". Our population had the highest numbers of people contracting AIDS.

Then people became not so afraid of it. Rather there grew to be an applauding in the number of our deaths. One less queer here on this earth. With no regard to anyone's heaven.

There became a new level of concern for one another in our world. We already were used to being told where we could not go, where we could not eat, where we could not shop, where we could not live, where we could not worship, where we could not work, where we could not serve, where we could not help, who we could not hug and that we don't love. So, we were used to being told of the nots and what nots!

This new epidemic of AIDS too tried to tear us apart within our own walls and amongst ourselves. It was not that we stopped loving each other, rather it was because we loved each other enough to want to preserve ourselves. Until we had some answers as to how this disease was spread, we chose to protect each other from getting it.

But for thousands it was too little too late. Privately, we watched each other die, one by one. These were not easy deaths to watch. Each was long and hard suffering. They went on for months and months. And for some, years even. And for those of us who were safe at least for the moment were still not sure how this disease was contracted so for any of us, at any time, we could be the next one to get it.

Because we did not know, caring for our dying was always a gamble. What would a hug do? What would a kiss do? What would a touch do? None of us knew but most all of us did it anyway. We were all scared but we did it anyway; out of love for one another!

Our pastors were not preaching so much anymore. Their voices were spent on the onslaught of memorial services and eulogies. And so many of our people died alone in hospital beds because partners and friends were forbidden in their rooms simply because they were gay. So many died alone without those who truly loved them beside them.

The tragic stories were innumerable and the grief was immense. Huge losses of life especially for those of us who remained.

There are two deaths that have impacted my life

the most; deaths due to AIDS. One was Terry the other one was Ken.

I was not close to Ken. I'm not quite sure if this was his name but this is the name I seem to remember so I will call him that.

Ken was a brother to a friend of mine, Connie. Connie was the partner of my best friend Carrie.

I actually knew nothing really of Ken till he started getting sick. I did not even meet him till the day I happened to be at Carrie and Connie's place. He was still on his feet back then but was very thin. Yet he still had a determination to live life. Then he took a turn for the worse and Connie had to start caring for him in her and Carrie's home.

I saw Ken again when he was still able to sit up in bed. But then ever so slowly Ken's organs began to fail him. The few times after that when I saw him, he was withering away. Ken got to the point where he needed twenty-four-hour care.

Carrie worked and went to school. Connie worked full time in a rehab facility. There came a time when they had to call on all their friends to come in and keep watch over Ken for them. We rotated around the clock. All of us. I was one of the least called. Ken just didn't know me. But I will never forget him.

As the weeks and months went on, the times I stayed with Ken were very difficult only because the watching of this body go from a good-looking guy to this ashen, sunken face. And a body that had wasted away to nothing but literally skin and bones. He always was in pain and all his dignity was stripped from him. I almost could not wait for him to die. And then he did.

Ken stands out to me for two reasons. The first is that Ken was the first long suffering death I had ever lived "bedside" with. The second is probably the most important and that was the testing of myself in regards to my own human compassion. I will be honest. I thought hard about sitting at his bedside, touching him, turning him over if needed, helping him if he needed to go. Ken was a mere stranger. Would it be worth it if he infected me?

My compassion won. Thank God!

The other death that I will never forget was that of Terry. I loved Terry. Other than his strong southern twang, everything about him reminded me of my brother Bob. He was soft spoken yet you knew he was in the room because of his big smile. He was a humble guy who would do anything for you. He always had his boots on with his jeans and of course his belt buckle. His shirt was always tucked in. You'd think he was a cowboy but I never saw him in a hat. Terry was the kind of guy you would never guess would die of this awful disease.

Terry's outbreak was different than any I had heard of before or even since. Terry was on vacation in New York and was at the airport waiting to board a plane to come home. He was there with his partner. As they were waiting Terry suddenly started bleeding through the arms of his shirt.

Terry got to an emergency room but it took days for him to be diagnosed. The bleeding was off and on, the bleeding through his skin. I believe it was several weeks before the hospital would release him to fly. They were afraid that the cabin pressure in the plane could accelerate any bleeding in him.

Terry did make it home. I saw Terry a few times after his return but it wasn't long after that Terry passed away. I was somewhat grateful I never saw Terry at his worst.

Terry left a partner behind. He wandered aimlessly in his grief over loosing Terry. He didn't even care if he might self-destruct.

As time went on and the numbers of our dead grew so did our hearts for one another. We all were full of grief for the living and the dead.

All of our living became so surreal. Things weren't supposed to be this way. Not even our normal was normal anymore. We all were numb. But something inside us came back to one thing we all knew and that was our unity. And survival.

So, we banned together in a celebration of the lives lost to AIDS. The Names Project was born. The AIDS Quilt was created. Anyone who lost someone to AIDS was invited to design a panel of their own honoring the memory of the one lost.

It was October 11, 1987 when the AIDS Quilt went

on display. I was there along with a half million other people.

This quilt grew to be massive; some nearly 2,000 panels. Just so many panels sown together to create a blanket of sorts. And each blanket displayed together covered the entire grounds overlooking our National Mall.

Each blanket was given enough space from the other to create a path for someone to walk beside each one and walk beside all four corners of each blanket.

One could never see in one day all the laying down of each one's life. A single square displayed there. The whole grounds were covered with them. But color, oh what color that covered the entire grounds there.

I will never forget the reverence I felt as I walked down each path, the solstice, the silence. We were united in life. Now here we stayed united in death.

That's just how we rolled!!!

RIP. Each and every one of you.

John 13:34-35 NLT

34 — So now I am giving you a new commandment: Love each other. Just as I have loved you, you should love each other.

35 — Your love for one another will prove to the world that you are My disciples.

PITTER
PATTER

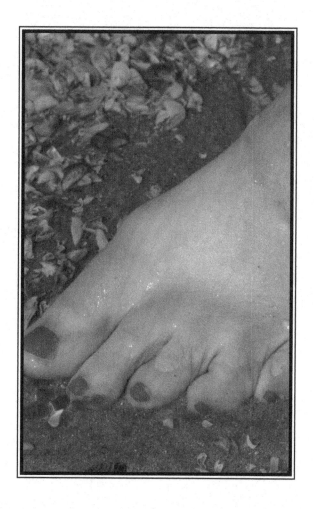

Blessed are those
who are humble...

PRIDE!

A funny word to use when thinking of those who are humble.

Maybe PRIDE was a bad choice of words. Maybe we should have used a word like glad or grateful.

We were glad when we could come out of our closets.

We were grateful we survived our basements.

Our chains were loosening its grip.

There was a new freedom on the horizon!

Yes, PRIDE was a very poor choice of words. But our PRIDE was different then the pride of all the rest of the world.

Our PRIDE came out of compassion; a different understanding of the human heart. We looked inside each other.

I believe all our so-called ranting was a cry out to the rest of the world to look inside us and to see all the good that was hidden there. We wanted you to see us and for you to get your eyes out from underneath our bed sheets.

Like the rest of the world, we had our great sinners like that. But mostly in the day in and the day out, there was nothing happening between our sheets.

We really were like everyone else. We just simply wanted to be loved. The only difference was that we had a different designers label than you.

We mostly all were a very meek people. We were

very well aware what the pride of the rest of the world could do to the human heart and the human soul. This pride, we wanted no part of it.

There was great compassion in us and we only cared to spread it around. We found ways to hold each other up. We formed community centers, resource centers, churches, art institutes, musicians, song writers, performers, artists, concerts, sports teams, festivals, support groups, business owners and so on and so on. We developed our own infrastructure; our own safety net. There was nothing outside our world that we would ever have to rely on. These were amazing days to be a part of and to live through.

We were ever so blessed. We were humbled by our ability, for the first time; to thrive.

I remember in the very early years of my finding my new family I went to the Michigan Women's Musical Festival. It was one of the first one's back then. This was a festival where women would get together for a long weekend and literally camp out. We were there to help each other out and get away from all our struggles. It was a safe place to meet and to exchange resources and to in the evenings listen to music together. There were many great artists of our kind who performed there.

The grounds that we stayed on was not very dense at all. And in the evenings as we all gathered to listen to the music, there was this astounding place. It was this huge bowl in the earth. I mean literally a bowl. I will never forget it. The stage was at the near rim of that bowl. I sat on the ground near the rim as well. I was to the left of the stage, midway to the front and the back of that bowl.

The evening was fairly young but it wasn't too long before the sun began to set behind the stage. The setting sun was a vast array of colors. It shortly after faded into darkness.

The darkness didn't last long before the sky lit up. It was so white that it had a hew of blue yet the shadows of the night still lingered in the sky. I remember thinking, "Where is this coming from?". I suddenly was more interested in the skies and the stars than I was in the songs being sung.

I kept watching the sky, then slowly but suddenly, a white bright light peaked over that bowl opposite the sunset. I had never seen a moon so large or so bright. It was huge, massive. It was so vast that it was as though I could reach out and touch it.

I was humbled to my knees. I saw it as a promise sign from God. That He was watching over us. That moon hoovered over us and showered us with a bright light. I will never forget it. I will never forget His promise there either.

Then darker days came upon us.

I had moved to San Francisco with my partner. This was where I escaped to when I fled from back home. It took us three days to get to San Francisco and once there we knew no one. When we hit town, we went to a gay resource center. Posted on the board there was this couple looking for roommates. So, we called and they came to meet us. Pat and Drena; Mischou and Denny as they were more fondly called.

We settled into their flat. Denny was an art framer and Mischou worked for the Gay Community Center.

We had arrived in San Francisco long after the assassinations of Harvey Milk and George Moscone. They were assassinated on November 27, 1978. Both men were the first openly gay elected officials in the United States. Both were assassinated by Dan White.

May 21, 1979 the sentencing for Dan White was handed out for the murder of Milk and Moscone. I slap on the wrist. Then all hell broke out.

The fighting began. We had had enough. After years of police brutality towards us in the streets and the raiding of our safe places with police badges that were cowardly covered over with black; now this. This assassin getting away with the murders of two of our people; we just could not take any more.

The four of us found ourselves in the midst of what history now calls "The White Night Riots".

That night we were all sitting around our kitchen table entrenched in what we were seeing on the news when Mischou got a call from the Gay Center informing her that there was a bomb threat at the Gay Center and could she get there.

All four of us got up and went. We were not even sure what we would run into even on our way to the

Center. We had seen that the streets were full of violence.

We made it to the Gay Center safely but inside was quite another thing. Practically no one else was there and it was eerily grey in every room we walked through. We weren't sure where to park ourselves and wait; to wait and see if the bomb threat was real or not. The only thing we knew was the time the bomb was due to go off.

So many things went through my mind as I waited. Nothing raced through my mind. Oddly, I had great peace in me. One thing that did roll over in my mind was that yes, I was willing to die if it meant those who would come after me that were of my kind, that maybe they would have a better life. Maybe they would have a better chance in this world. Yes, I was prepared to die.

Watching. Waiting. Knowing. Not knowing. Watching the seconds tic off the clock. Waiting for the next minute to pass. Knowing I was prepared to die. Not knowing if I would.

The room was still a very eerie grey.

It was time. The last tic of the clock hit that moment in time. We were all still and seemingly without breath.

Then boom – complete silence! The clock kept ticking.

We looked at each other not daring to breathe. Was it really over and what had we just done!?

The realization that we all could be dead. The realization that the four of us were willing to die.

Amazing grace!

My stories are endless. The promises of God and how He has carried me.

My feet have touched many a soil across this land of ours. My eyes have seen the magnificence of God in all that I saw. But there is only one thing that I treasure more than anything and that is all the kindness that was poured out from the hearts of my people.

There was a gathering up of each other and a holding unto each other like I had never known before. I miss those days.

Our greatest enemy became the scattering of ourselves. When the pride of the world became our heart's desire.

Our humble stepping turned into a strut.

I don't know. Since I've been back home with my blood family, I have been far away from my other family, my community; maybe I need to visit them if only to test my own heart.

Am I humble enough to give back to them? To teach them what all I have learned through my life? To tell them the history of all their origins? To say to them "I remember the day when…"? To tell them the stories of all the history I hold in my hands?

Who will tell them? Who will tell them the truth? Who will teach them of all we suffered through? Who will tell them of the long hard road that was paved for them so that they might be better off today? Who will be sure to keep alive the remembrance of all the suffering and persecution that went on long before them?

And who will teach them of this greater love we had for one another? Who?

Who will listen to their struggles of today?

Yes, the world is more tolerant of us today but I'm not so sure that this does not come at a price all its own.

Early on we had to be bold. We had to be loud. We had to march. We had to do many things before anyone would hear our cries to be loved. Now that everyone has heard our cries, there is still very little love for us.

This is the blur this next generation of my people is having to live in. Sure, the world know sees us. Everyone now knows we exist. Despite the world we now can let our lights shine in the world. But something is still missing.

Yes, we can now blend with the rest of the world but this is not at all what we were initially seeking. We were seeking to be loved by the rest of the world. This is the very spot our next generation is still trapped in. The longing to be loved. That longing that has yet to be fulfilled. There is a vast difference between blending and belonging; a mere tolerance and a joining together.

Maybe there is no such thing or maybe in some ways we have gone way too far in seeking to be loved by those outside of us. Our desire to blend at the sacrifice of our belonging to each other.

Did the slow suffocation of our lives by those outside

of us finally give us our last breath? Did we finally wave the white flag and surrender? Did we just become so weary of the fight to simply be loved? Was it just not worth the fight anymore?

I am no expert but I do know that I was there when we walked away from the fight.

I know what my heart tells me. And that is that God has given me a good heart, a tender heart. A heart of great compassion and that of deep sorrow. This I would not surrender.

My heart has always seemed right within me. Maybe it was my vision that got in my way.

I know I am to bring light into darkness wherever I go.

I know I must leave a lasting imprint no matter my journey.

I know I must not spare my love from anyone no matter how different they are from me. This one should be easy. That means to love everyone because there is no one just like me. Huh!

I must be the pitter patter of the Spirit and like a whispering in the wind so that the stomping of all humanity settles into silence.

With all that I am and with everything that is in me; I must love.

The delicate slow dance of life.

Ecclesiastes 3:1-8 NLT

For everything there is a season, a time for every activity under heaven.

A time to be born and a time to die.

A time to plant and a time to harvest.

A time to kill and a time to heal.

A time to tear down and a time to build up.

A time to cry and a time to laugh.

A time to grieve and a time to dance.

A time to scatter stones and a time to gather stones.

A time to embrace and a time to turn away.

A time to search and a time to quit searching.

A time to keep and a time to throw away.

A time to tear and a time to mend.

A time to be quiet and a time to speak.

A time to love and a time to hate.

A time for war and a time for peace.

Ecclesiastes 3:11 NLT

Yet God has made everything beautiful for its own time. He has planted eternity in the human heart, but even so, people cannot see the whole scope of God's work from beginning to end.

LEPERS AND THE LEFT BEHIND

Blessed are those who
hunger and thirst...

There grew this warfare in me.

This started at a very young age. I did not understand it. After all, there seemed to be a sense of safety all around me but inside of me, I was very aware of a lurking danger. I somehow knew that what was in me was not safe outside of me, at least not at home.

For some reason I did not do well with the "saved" ones. It was the broken and lost that I was always drawn to. Strangers became the magnet to my living and seemed to be what held me together.

This was the place where I lived most of my life. Some would call it that parodical place. I call it my walk with God. Something inside me told me that I was not the one lost as I was made to believe. Rather, I grew into this awareness that I seemed to be the one found.

I came from a very dried up place. I left to find water. I found water through the wilderness of this world.

A celebration began in me. A freedom like I had never known. That darkness began to fade away and a light began to shine in me. I became different. I was finally away from all that scapegoating put on my life.

I was finally set free from that heritage of pride. That heritage of pretending that all is well. That heritage of burying one's head in the sand. That heritage of perfection. That heritage of deep dark secrets and lies. That heritage of violation to another's innocent body. I left to create a new heritage.

I thank God that He gave me the gumption, the courage, to leave my roots. To live outside of all I knew.

Then and there I was free to discover the heart that was in me. The cuts to my soul might have a chance to mend. And the filthy minds were now left behind.

I was free now to seek for myself, to find my own answers, to discover truth. I was no longer looking to others for answers. I sought after the heavenlies. The blindness in my eyes began to peel away. I began to see things through the eyes of God.

God was no longer apart from this earth but rather my God became a part of all this world with me. But even more, within me.

Black and white began to fade away and color began to fill my world.

I have experienced many things in my walk thru life. I have seen many things in my life. I have learned that nothing is totally dark here on this earth and that nothing is totally light here either. And that everything has a seed whether meant for good or meant for evil.

One thing I did not witness, but it tore my heart up as if I had been a witness; it is the true story of this one man's death that actually brought a resemblance to the death of Jesus.

His name was Matthew Shepard, a gay man. He was kidnapped, robbed and beaten and strapped to a ranch fence. He was left there to die.

Matthew hung on that fence for 18 hours before he was ever spotted there. Once spotted, Matthew was cut free only to die five days later in the hospital.

How can one make sense of all the nonsense in

all our humanity? All the hate over being different. But different than what?

The free fall of all our humanity.

We are taught that God remembers our every good deed and yes, He does. But I have also learned that my sins too are very personal to God.

Does He forgive my sins? Oh, yes of course or the cross would not have been necessary. But I believe it truly grieves God when we sin especially when it involves hurting one another.

"Jesus wept!"

I was raised in a Christian Reformed Church where the casting out of sinners was far greater than any welcoming in of anyone who was "beneath" us. There truly was not much of God's Kingdom there other than the wrath of God through the judgement from the pulpit and the pews.

I will never forget sitting in those pews in my youth and early teens. When it came the day of communion how saddened I was that I was not allowed to participate. I wanted to drink the wine and eat the bread so I could participate in the sacrifice Jesus made for me. Being excluded made me feel like Jesus didn't die for me. That Jesus died only for the grown ups in those pews. I felt left behind.

Then came time for my "Profession of Faith". I truly felt God in me. He was stirring in my life.

Profession of Faith was a ritual in the church that

actually made you a member of that church. It was expected of every teenager if you wanted to stay in that church.

I truly wanted to profess my faith in front of everyone in that church, not to become a member, but because I wanted to profess to them the work God was doing in me.

In order to stand before the church and profess my faith, I went through all the rituals to be approved in order to do so. The day that I did stand and profess, there was a celebration of sorts. I went to the basement of that church were the celebration was being held. Lo and behold there on that table was this small box with my name on it containing tithing envelopes. I felt betrayed.

Is this what mattered most to the church? Was it not my spiritual walk that should have been tended to rather than my purse strings? Should it have been a greater concern to the church where I stood with God rather than their rituals and my money? Was there no giving back to God other than money?

No wonder I hate money. No wonder I don't belong to a church institution.

I had come back home to live after being gone for thirty years. I am very close to my two sisters, Sharon and Diane. One day in a conversation the three of us were having, my sister Diane called me a Christian. I think my shoulders jerked from being taken so aback. I was repulsed even. I had been called many things in my life but Christian was not one of them. I carried many labels in my life, some of them were true. But to be called a Christian?!! I didn't quite know what to do with this one.

Christians. Weren't they the ones that cast me out? Weren't they the ones who said I was demon possessed? Weren't they the ones who wouldn't claim me as their own? Weren't they the ones that told me if I didn't get back to church, I would lose my job? Weren't they the ones that told me, God does not love me? Weren't they the ones that said I could never be saved? Weren't they the ones who ripped my life to shreds?

There was no good Samaritan in any Christian I had ever met!

I would rather be a Christ follower than a Christian. There, this was my new name; Follower! Follower of Jesus!

I wanted off the broad path of exclusion. And yes, the broad path leads to destruction. I sought after the narrow path that leads me only to God. The path where He and I alone walk. The path that leads to room at the table.

I was questioned by this pastor once who had a curiosity in, we homosexuals. Seems there were some in his church struggling with it. He asked me "What gives them the right to form their own church for their own specific sexual sins?" He was referring to the

MCC churches around the world. The "homosexual church" as it is referred to by man.

I simply replied to this pastor, "Because your church threw us out!"

If I was in the mood for warfare, I would have said to him, "And what gives you the right, oh sinner, to be a pastor over sinners of every other kind of sin except ours?" I kept my mouth shut.

Will you who sit on the throne of your pulpits lead sheep just to add or subtract to your flock or will you tend to the business of never leaving a single sheep left behind?

Or will it be the lepers who only add to the fold?

It still grieves me to my core when this gay man said to me "I know I'm going to hell – there is a special spot there for me with my name on it." I know this brainwashing very well. It doesn't change anyone's nature here on earth. It only casts one into a deeper despair and turns one away from God.

Why would one say to the suffering, "Are you saved?" or why would one say to a suffering one "You can never be saved."?

We at least knew our sin. How could we not. It was plastered everywhere. The sins of those not like us however, remain locked in closets.

We made no excuses for our sin. So many of us had salvation in us and were simply walking out our sanctification.

Does it take the so-called unsaved ones to teach those who pridefully claim to be the saved ones?

Be ever so careful of the white-washed; seems there is no blood in them.

There was this man, Robert who worked for an outside vendor at my place of business. Robert was an extremely spiritual man. I worked in this isolated room away from everyone else in the company so it gave us great opportunity to talk about anything we wanted to. Robert was rich in knowledge of the Word of God especially pertaining to Jesus. If he didn't say it once, he said it a thousand times in my at least five years of knowing him, "I love Christ Jesus, my Savior and Lord!".

I always looked forward to the day Robert would be in. Robert was full of wisdom and knowledge. I learned so much from him but I also surprised myself in how much I knew of God's Word. When we would talk together, we were elevated on a plain that seemed to be above even the two of us.

I learned from Robert and Robert learned from me.

We talked much about the end days, the rapture, the signs of the times, what was going on in the world that day and what it might mean going forward. Robert also predicted that the year 2020 would be a very pivotal year, and that great and lasting changes were coming.

Robert gave me many a CD of the preaching of God's Word. He ministered at a truck stop on his days off. I often asked him why he didn't become a pastor. He simply replied "I was meant to be like Jesus; one by one."

One thing I did learn about Robert and that in his deep love and passion for Christ Jesus he developed a god-like syndrome. He took it upon himself to develop levels of salvation; the do's and don'ts of it. There was this selective covering of sins in his mind.

So many times, in all our discussions Robert would bring up the homosexuals and how they especially would not be saved. My tongue still bleeds from all my tongue biting. And every time I felt my face flush with a quiet rage. But I said nothing.

I learned to manage my hurt, frustration and lack of retaliation by telling myself over and over again, that one day when I knew that our business relationship was near an end I would turn to Robert and say, "I just want you to know, you've been talking to a homosexual all these years." I just couldn't wait for that day. I just couldn't wait to hear what he might say. I just couldn't wait to see the look on his face.

That day never came.

Oh, maybe two months ago I got a call from Vince a co-worker of Roberts. This was on a Tuesday. He told me that Robert had "just fell out" at a dealership he was working at.

That Friday I received another call from Vince. Robert was going to be taken off all life support. There had been no brain activity since his fall on Tuesday.

Gone. Gone in an instant. Taken. It reminded me of the rapture we spoke so much about.

Yes Robert, you were right. 2020 was a very pivotal year for you!

Maybe now he knows that I am a homosexual.

Things unseen!

A foolish man once said to me, "If I didn't see it; if I were not there, then it never happened."

I could only reply, "Does this include the cross?"

Oh, foolish man!
Do you have no faith?

Foolish man!
Do you not believe?

Oh, foolish man!
Do you not see?

John 15:18-19 NLT

18 – If the world hates you, remember that it hated Me first.

19 – The world would love you as one of its own if you belonged to it, but you are no longer part of the world. I chose you to come out of the world, so it hates you.

THE MOONE
AND A STARR

*Blessed are those
who are merciful...*

Every act of giving has a memory. So, too every act of help has a memory. So, too every act of kindness has a memory. So, too every act of compassion has a memory. None of these will be left to waste in the Kingdom of God.

Proverbs 11:30 NLT says, "The seeds of good deeds become a tree of life..."

Here is my story of the two greatest beings in all my life; my two greatest teachers. They both have four legs. Moone and Starr.

Moone was a full-sized, medium brown boxer with a white marking on his crown. He had black markings that accented parts of his legs but especially around his eyes and snout.

Starr was a who knows what. I picked Starr up from out of a box of puppies at a flee market in Alabama. Her tail had a white tip on it. A sign that she was some kind of a hunter dog. Starr had a white star like shape on her crown; thus, her name.

I brought Starr back to my home outside Atlanta, Georgia. Starr grew to be a medium sized dog. She was a light tan with flecks of white and black that accented her body. Her eye brows and snout were especially black.

I grew fast in my love for Starr from the moment I picked her up from out of that box to every single moment after that. Starr had something different in her. She was not an ordinary dog like those that I had before her. Starr knew something. There seemed to be an awareness in her that not even most human beings had. She was so keen. It was like she knew something. It was like she knew of something else.

I had a stake in my back yard that had a very long line that Starr could run on. She loved the outdoors. There also was this tree stump in my back yard. Starr loved to stand on it with all four of her legs. She would perch there and howl and look into the heavens. She reigned there. Starr was like no other.

Then Starr met Moone.

Moone, the boxer, was a rescue dog that a co-worker of mine adopted. She had a different name for him that I can't even recall now. So, he will be referred to by my new name for him, Moone.

Here is Moone's story. Moone was owned and held captive by this drug dealer. He was chained up in the yard and neglected. He was only there to fend people off or scare them away and warn his owner that someone was near. Then something horrific happened.

Moone was struck in the head with an axe. It went in between his ears. Moone was still chained up and on the brink of death when the authorities found him. The authorities resuscitated Moone and were able to save him. Moone was not only scarred above his crown, he was scarred in his soul and spirit.

Moone would nor could no longer bark. He would wake up randomly through the night with his head bent and twisted and walk in circles as if still in chains. If there was such a thing as animals having hope, he had none. He had no joy in him either. He was no longer chained but lived as though he was. He was so very nervous. He was present but seemed lost in nowhere.

As God would have it, this co-worker and I began to share our ride to work together. She had a wooded, large fenced in back yard. She would leave Moone out there while we were at work. This greatly troubled me since Georgia summers could be so brutally hot. Yes, this back yard was very shaded yet my tender heart could just not stand Moone out there all alone.

So, I offered to bring Starr over to stay with Moone while we were at work all day. This was fine. When we would get back from work each day, I would first replenish their water dishes then I would begin to frolic with them. Starr would have a blast. Moone just watched until one day he started to frolic a little too. Then the day came when Moone swung into a down right dance. He would have the time of his life each time we came home from work.

Moone's lost look, his empty eyes began to show signs of light. Moone's lifelessness began to grow into joy.

Summer was drawing near. I knew that I could not leave Starr out in the heat even in the shade. So, I offered to have Moone come stay inside at my house to be with Starr. By now they were getting rather inseparable. This became fine. So, Starr and Moone stayed together at my place during the day.

Before long, the days together turned into nights together and I'm not even quite sure how this happened but then Moone became mine and Starr and Moone were together night and day. The three of us would play together indoors and out. Starr would bark with joy. Moone watched everything that Starr would do. He began to be a dog again and did he ever begin to bark. Eventually even Moone's nightmares began to fade away until there was no more circling in chains in the middle of the night. Starr taught Moone all of these things. Starr taught Moone how to be a dog maybe for the first time in his life.

Starr was Moone's star and Moone was Starr's moon. They filled the sky with their love for one another.

I eventually moved back home to Grand Rapids, Michigan. Moone was getting not old but up there in years. His hips were giving out on him and I knew I had to put him down. What a rotten day that was. I made the decision to bring Starr along in the car. A huge mistake. Starr knew.

The people at the vet had to help get Moone out of the car. Starr went nuts! Starr fought with all her might not to let anyone take Moone. Her cries were that of terror. I never heard anything like it before. I hurt so bad with her and for her. It took years for Starr to shake that panic from her. That fright in her never left her. It was in her eyes for a very long time. She was never again the same in that blue Honda of mine.

A part of Starr died when Moone left this earth. Home felt so empty and Starr just could not quite recover. Starr had little life in her and I could not stand it.

Starr was so unusual. She was full of love and now had nowhere to put it. I was not enough for her. Starr was a teacher in her world. She needed a new student.

In comes Badger. A six-year-old. The same age as Starr. Badger was a Labrador, German Shepherd mix.

Well Starr? Be careful what you wish for.

Badger was a fire cracker. Everything ignited him. At six years old, Badger was like a puppy on steroids. There was no such thing as walking him. I would have lost my chin in the dirt years ago. Thank God for my fenced in back yard. And Badger's bark, well it was so load and deep that it shook my walls.

I have a big living room window and every time someone would walk by; Badger would literally climb up the window. His claw marks are still embedded in that glass window today. Needless to say, Starr had her work cut out for her.

Starr being Starr, she worked at Badger little by little and Badger began to calm the storm within him.

One of my favorite seasons to watch the two of them in was in the winter. They both loved the snow. They would race together across the long yard towards the shed. If Badger would get out of line Starr would tug at him near his ear. They were beautiful to watch together, side by side. If they could have, I'm sure they would have had great snowball fights together. I could see it in their eyes.

Starr was, is and always will be this earth's lucky star. If mercy could be measured, she surely would have tipped the scales. She definitely did her part to hold the world around her up. I will never forget the trembling in her legs when she could no longer hold herself up.

And I will never forget that after Starr's passing, the memory Badger had of her. Badger would mourn by peacefully laying in the grass and look up to the heavens as if he could see her there.

Starr loved to lay in the grass. She would search with her eyes for all that was around her just as a shepherd would do. Then one day I noticed that her sights had changed. Her eyes were no longer looking to all that was around her. Instead she was now looking up into the heavens more and more. Her eyes gazed into the sky. It was as if she knew, something was waiting on her.

I will never forget this one particular day as Starr laid on that hill between those two bushes as she watched me from a distance rake the leaves. Our eyes locked and neither could let go. I knew in those moments that it would not be long before Starr would be watching me from heaven.

Soon after, the day came when Starr just stopped eating. I tried everything, anything to get her to eat.

She just would not eat. I remember yelling at her in fear, "Starr if you don't eat you are going to die!". Days turned into weeks. Starr was over sixteen now and I knew heaven was calling her home. I knew it and it hurt like…!!! I prayed for days that God grant Starr in her death the same mercy she had given in all her living. God's assignment for Starr's life was nearing an end.

I asked for mercy in Starr's dying and God answered my prayers.

I was looking out my kitchen window, Badger and Starr were outside. It was an early evening, nearing the end of a bright sunny day. Starr was standing in the grass at the edge of the concrete slab. I saw Starr's four legs suddenly collapse underneath her. She was grabbing this earth with all that was in her. She looked up at the window to me and looked terrified. I ran outside and scooped Starr up. I was given extra strength, I know. I got her in the car and took her to the emergency clinic.

We were put in a room and in that room, Starr clung to me like never before. I knew she was so very scared but I also knew she put her trust in me like never before.

They came in for Starr and Starr reluctantly went. They had to put a catheter in her so they could put her down. When they brought Starr back and set her on the floor, she came racing towards me. I was kneeling. I then laid on the floor and Starr laid next to me snuggling as close as she could. I held her tight and embraced her with all my heart, weeping as I kissed her over and over again on that star on her crown. I never wanted to let go of her. She clung to me and I clung to her.

I kept telling Starr through my tears that she would now be with Moone and that one day I would be with them both. I told her to go and be with Moone once again and that Moone was waiting on her. Then she quietly and gently did. The star on her crown was soaked from all my tears.

I will miss her till forever!

On April 20th God confirmed to me with His big moon in the sky and its wondrous reflection on that river that Moone and Starr were united forever. They are not resting. They are frolicking forever more.

Mercy is as mercy does.

Then came Gabby. A miniature English Shepherd. I picked her up on a Good Friday and on a full moon. Gabby was twelve years old at the time. She was growing deaf and blind. Badger didn't mind. All he wanted was some company once again. He knew there would never be another Starr.

I must tell this one brief story. I am a student of this very great teacher in my life about life. Her name is Jan. Jan is no longer here on this earth. She died of a rare form of breast cancer.

Jan taught me two great things. One thing she taught me was to live life with passion. Jan lived a very robust life full of joy and full of passion. She always was happy. I don't think I ever saw her without a smile on her face. Everything about her was welcoming.

The other thing Jan taught me was to live a zealous life of generosity. Jan always had an open hand. Jan took great pleasure in it. Her heart was full of mercy for those in need and even for those without a need. This was Jan. This was who she was.

I was told of one of Jan's greatest messages left behind nearing her last years. There was this beggar on the street corner and Jan reached out to hand him a twenty-dollar bill. The passenger in astonishment said, "What are you doing? Who knows what he will spend it on!"? Jan answered back, "It's between him and God in how he spends it. What matters is that I give it to him."

What a teaching. To have compassion. To have compassion even while not knowing its end result.

Compassion is not intentional.

Compassion is instinctive.

Who says no one is watching?
Who says no one is paying attention?

Proverbs 19:17 NLT says, "If you help the poor, you are lending to the Lord - and He will repay you!"

James 2:8-9 NLT

8 — Yes indeed, it is good when you obey the royal law as found in the scriptures: "Love your neighbor as yourself."

9 — But if you favor some people over others, you are committing a sin. You are guilty of breaking the law.

WHIRLY BIRDS

Blessed are those whose
hearts are pure...

The wind blows and blows without end.

This is the breath of the Spirit.

These are the earth angels.

That breeze that only belongs to God. There is no lesser than or greater than here.

I must tell you this story. Julie Clark was a landlord of mine. When I was ready to move back to Grand Rapids, Michigan, Julie took me in sight unseen, from out of state, unemployed and with my many animals. Julie owned a duplex. She lived on one side and I was to rent the other side.

When I first saw Julie, I thank God I didn't judge her by the standards of this world. Julie was pale and she had straggly hair and bulging eyes. Her belly was filled out as if she were pregnant. Julie was very timid but she welcomed me with a very sweet smile and always when she saw me, she would do a slight curtsy. Julie was always soft-spoken and was she ever tender-hearted.

I found out later that Julie was Miss Grand Rapids in her youth. I saw a photo of her from those days and she was absolutely stunning. I would never have guessed that the woman who stood before me was the same woman in those photos. As time went on and I got to know Julie more and more, the only thing that could have changed her from where she was back then to where she was now, was the tenderness in Julie's heart.

Julie's mother shared often with me stories of how

when Julie was young, when she would see a child, if she had food in her hand, Julie would feed that child. Julie was always caring for others, especially children. Julie cared so much for others that she let her own life go. Julie wasted herself away from the agony in her own broken heart.

Julie's health was not good and she was in and out of the hospital. I would visit her and sit on the side of her bed. Often times I would brush her hair aside and kiss her on the forehead and tell her I loved her.

What came out of me in those days took me by surprise. I normally am more planned and calculated but with Julie there came out of me a natural flow of love. An unquestionable expression towards her. I knew I was tender inside but for the first time in my life, caring for Julie came purely from my instincts.

Julie's elderly father passed away and her mother was left alone in their home. Julie still was not well herself so she went to stay with her mother. This left Julie's side of the duplex unattended and the property as a whole unattended too. I became the "landlord" and watched over the land and property while still remaining a renter.

Julie was gone for months at a time. One day, with no other choice I had to enter Julie's side. What a mess! It could have easily been condemned.

Instead, Julie hired a clean-up crew. They brought in a dumpster that took up the whole long length of the driveway, all the way to the street. The clean-up took weeks. I saw Julie more in those weeks than I had in the last year; her and her mother both. They wanted to keep everything that was thrown into that dumpster. They were both either too weak or too old to take back much of anything.

Julie had this piano and bench in her living room. On one of her visits back to the duplex Julie came running next door to me raising a ruckus. Her piano bench was gone. I went next door and sure enough the piano bench was gone; thrown in that dumpster with everything else she owned.

Then there was Julie's garage door opener. She looked everywhere at her mothers and in their vehicles and back at her place. I even went over to her mother's several times to help Julie look for it. It was nowhere to be found. I could testify to that.

Time passed and so too did Julie. Julie passed several months after all of this. It's a long story but God provided a way for me to purchase Julie's duplex, as is. We, my friend Jan and I had great plans for what was Julie's side. A tribute of sorts to all of Julie's lovingkindness.

I came home after the closing on the property. Of course, I had left everything locked up tight as a drum in my absence. There is a double garage between the two sides of the duplex. I entered what was Julie's side through the garage entry. Lo and behold, when I took those two steps into the kitchen, there sat Julie's garage door opener neatly placed on the corner of that kitchen counter. I was flabbergasted.

It didn't end there. I walked through the hall from the

kitchen that led to the living room. I couldn't believe my eyes when I rounded the corner into the living room. There sat that piano bench perfectly tucked beneath the piano. My jaw dropped and my eyes popped wide open.

If this wasn't confirmation from God...!

Yes, God can and will use anything, even a garage door opener and a piano bench to remind me that He can and will move and shuffle things around according to His will and purpose. Reminding me that He and His angels are watching over me and that they are all around me.

But, oh, me of little faith. I back tracked with everyone, those that cleaned Julie's side out and the realtor and my friend Jan. All had witnessed that the piano bench had been gone. Besides, no one had access to that side to bring that bench back even if they had taken it. That piano bench was not there when we left for closing. Jan and I both knew it had been long gone. But even still we examined the spindles on the legs of that piano bench and compared them to the spindles on the legs of that piano. A perfect match.

And the garage door opener, only I knew about it being lost.

Yes, God does truly work in mysterious ways. God owns and is in charge of everything.

I learned my lesson.

But I should not have been surprised at any of these things.

Even as a child, I had a sense of the presence of God. It was such a different thing than what I saw that was going on all around me. I was there yet I was not. There seemed to be something between me and all the rest of the world. It wasn't a bad thing it was just this degree of separation between me and all the rest of this world. It was just this odd place.

I remember standing on this mound of the school yard where I went to elementary school. It was on this day that had been predicted that the world would come to an end at a specific time on that day. I stood on that mound and bravely looked to the heavens, waiting. It seemed as if God was with me and that the end would not come. I was OK there, in that moment.

I remember as a kid I used to play marbles. I don't think it was so much for the sport of it as it was for all the colors in them. But here too, there seemed to be something there between me and that ground.

I played a lot of sports growing up and in my teens. I wasn't the best but I wasn't that bad either. I never understood why I could not more fully connect between me and the ball or me and that hoop. In that last second there was something that pulled me back. It was very frustrating to me. I could have been a great player if it weren't for this thing. But I seemed to have no control over it.

In hindsight now so many things make more sense to me. I think I have always been more engaging with the spirit in me rather than the other parts of me. I really believe this began from my mother's womb and how I almost didn't make it out. God and I must have been in a fierce battle together in order to make this happen. How can one get any closer to God than this; other than to die!

I believe this fight with God for my life, not against God, is what has sealed our bond together. And has kept me closer to Him than anything else on this earth. An almost sacred place.

I also believe because of this I have an extra pair of eyes, spiritual eyes.

The Spirit of God has always been keen in me. But this has brought an added responsibility. A deeper pricking to my soul over what is good and what is evil.

So, with this extra thing how would I make my life most matter? What will I teach others? What will others learn from me? What will I be taught from others? What will I learn? What kind of difference will I have made? What part of God's tapestry will I have sown my threads into?

How will I know my life mattered? How will I know that what others have seen in me, that I have represented my Maker well?

How can I be sure I did not snuff the Spirit out of another? What did I do to prevent the Spirit from being snuffed out of me?

God gave me a few glimpses along the way.

There was this young man Zach at the place where I worked. He was a young buck who had suffered many hard things already in his young life. I had many long talks with Zach and on many occasions, he hung unto my every word. I shared with him many of my own life lessons along the way. Some were simply practical. Others were deeper. And some were having to do with right and wrong. He paid attention and was hungry to learn.

Zach later shared with me, "Marcia, the things you have taught me will remain with me for the rest of my life." He said at another time, "Marcia, you need to write another book. You need to write a book on your life stories." It did my heart good to know I had impacted Zach to this degree.

Zach was so cute. He would pop up out of nowhere throughout the day and ask me, "So, Marcia tell me another story."

My workplace has always been a good measuring stick, a mirror even, for what I was or was not doing right in life. Sometimes it is in an "out of the blue" statement. This man at work said to me, "You are a whisperer not a complainer." Wow. People really do pay attention.

Don't get me wrong. I am in no way a saint. The work place has also tested and tried the dark side in me as well. You know the scripture about loving your enemy and pray for those who persecute you. Well, this side of the coin did not set well with me. I had a lot to learn on this subject and about the resistance in me to put this kind of loving into practice.

Have you ever come across someone who is so kind and genuine in the beginning then one day like a flip of a switch, a deep darkness takes hold of them?

I knew a man like this. Navigating this change was a tough place to be in. I wanted, watched and waited for the good in this man to return. But instead when that darkness set in so too the battle between him and I.

This man just spewed contempt for me. He did wear me out and most of my day was spent in spiritual warfare with him. It sucked out nearly all the good energy I had in me. This went on for years. He became the picture of, "Pray for your enemies."

I finally decided in my mind one day and even chuckled at the thought, "Man, don't you ever get tired of thinking about me?"

A new manager came in and after dealing with this guy for some time turned to me and said, "I don't pray much but I sure do pray for him." I replied back, "I have fought him so much that I can't even pray for him anymore."

In one of our last verbal battles, this guy lashed out at me and had the gull to say to me, "And you call yourself a Christian!" I had never once called myself that; not in the work place. But maybe if in his mind; if I was opposite him then I must be a Christian. Or maybe it was all the warfare I refused to engage in with him; maybe that is what made him call me a Christian. Only God knows.

All I know for sure is this man is out of my life. He

is no longer employed there at that place of business. He has gone on to who knows where. I can only pray that he carries with him a different spirit.

I had gotten my nephew a job where I worked; this same place of business. Not long after he started, he asked me if I were gay. He told me that my co-workers had told him that I was. I asked back, "Is that all they said about me? They didn't have worse things to say about me?" He replied, "No, they didn't say anything else about you." I pondered this within me, so they had no good thing or no bad thing to say about me; only that I was gay. I was amazed this was all they had said of me since so many painted me as their enemy. My standards had always seemed too high for some of them. At least in their eyes.

My last reply to my nephew was, "Always seek the truth."

My nephew had no idea that I was gay until that day. This hurt. It only meant that I was still the shame of the family.

The wind blows.

There have been tender glimpses of the reflections of my life.

In one of my father's hospital stays he shared this with me through his tears. He said that he wished that he had lived bolder for God. He added that even as an elder and a deacon in the church he wished he had been bold enough to tell more people about God. What a confession I thought.

My dad read the Bible beautifully and faithfully. And his prayers were, well; I'm sure it was easy work for Jesus to refine them before He presented them to God.

After this confession, I had to step back for a moment. This was personal to me.

My parents had always been very hard on me, the one they seemed most judgmental of. I was never the conforming type. But in this moment, I felt my dad making some sort of amends to me.

My father then reached out his hand and touched the bag I was carrying and with a slight smile on his face, he said to me, "So, is this your purse?" I smiled back and with a finger to my lips replied back, "Shhh... You don't want to ruin my reputation." A moment of redemption. What a precious moment.

On 12/29/2012, my dad turned to me and said, "You have taught us many things." I was ever so humbled.

The wind still blows.

And every flutter in life matters. Whether for good or for evil.

I believe I had briefly mentioned earlier about my job being threatened if I did not go back to church. This was the first real job I had coming out of high school.

My upbringing and all of the community around me were that of a very rigid Christian Reformed Church.

The owner of this jewelry store was no different. He let me know in no uncertain terms that if I wanted to keep my job, I must go back to church.

That never happened and as suddenly as I left home, I left that job without warning and never looked back.

Over forty years later, now moved back home. My parents were having an anniversary celebration and this retired jewelry store owner was there. When he saw me, he walked up to me and said, "I want to apologize for the wrong I did you." I graciously and humbly accepted his apology.

It was not long after that, that Bill passed away.

The inner eye. That eye-gate.

Angels do watch over us.

True story.

My brother Harry and a few other guys were out cruising down this road in the dark of the night. All of them completely sober. They were speeding down this two-lane road at over 100 miles per hour. Suddenly, right in front of their eyes was this cow in the middle of the road immediately ahead of them. In that split second, they knew there was nothing they could do. They would all surely die.

They could do nothing but go with what was the inevitable. Then in an instant, that cow was picked up from off the road and placed in a field beside the road and behind a fence. All were spared!

I would have loved to have been in that car the

moments after to see the look on each one's face and to hear all the, "Did you see that???" that were spoken.

Things unseen.

The unexplainable!

The eyes of God are everywhere.

I remember this one spring day when my spirit was being quenched, I looked out my windows and walked out my back door. Whirly birds were everywhere. I had never seen so many showered unto my land. They covered the grass and kept twirling down from above.

My first thought after witnessing the beauty of them was, "How am I ever going to get all of these cleaned up?".

Then I heard the whisper and a big smile came over my face. All these whirly birds were a promise to me sent by God. God's wink at me. Then a knowing welled up in me that what I was working on was right in the eyes of God. I kept smiling.

Ecclesiastes 11:5 NLT "Just as you cannot understand the path of the wind or the mystery of a tiny baby growing in its mother's womb, so you cannot understand the activity of God, who does all things."

Isaiah 55: 8-9 NLT "My thoughts are nothing like your thoughts," says the Lord. "And My ways are far beyond anything you could imagine. For just as the heavens are higher than the earth, so My ways are higher than your ways and My thoughts higher than your thoughts."

The sound of the whistle train!
All is well.

John 3:8 NLT

The wind blows wherever it wants. Just as you can hear the wind but can't tell where it comes from or where it is going, so you can't explain how people are born of the Spirit.

FLESH, BLOOD AND BEYOND

Blessed are those who work for peace...

Melanin. The body's natural coloring; pigment found in the skin, hair, eyes, inner ears and other parts.

Melanin. Not a choice in any of us.

Laminin. That single molecule that holds all of our being together. Not a choice either.

All of us combined are like the colors of the rainbow. Each one alone is created with a natural born cross throughout their being.

There is only one single thing that no matter where you are in the spectrum of the rainbow or no matter what you do with your naturally born cross, there still is only one thing we all share. That is the color of our blood.

We all bleed red.

Our red blood is the only DNA that makes us all from one heritage. It is the signature of our Creator.

My mother once told me of this wise woman who asked, "Have you ever wondered what it would be like if snow were any other color than white? Can you imagine if snow were the color of red?"

What if our blood was white and snow was red?

That would be real backwards. Don't we, our sins have to be as scarlet before they can be as white as snow?"

And how would the blood of Jesus ever fit in? I know when He shed His blood on the cross that His blood was red. How could He have died in our place if our blood was not red like His?

Red blood puts the all in us, even Jesus.

ALL. Amazingly Linked Likeness.

We all have the red blood in us. This cannot be changed. But what in us can be changed? How about our hearts?

Can one's heart be measured on a scale? Can one side balance the measure of love while the other side balance the measure of hate?

Aren't these the only two things that matter in our hearts; love or hate?

Tribes and nations. The battlefields in all humanity. My tribe was no exception; the homosexual tribe.

There grew to be a genocide awaiting my tribe from all the other nations. As on all battlefields, most of us turned into great warriors. Many lost their lives in the fight. Many took their lives because of the fight.

We never wanted to be at war. We simply wanted to be. We knew we were "flawed" before anyone had ever told us. We lost many a battle from the war within. We didn't need anyone's help. Most of us were in an agony all on our own.

Arrows were coming from both sides; the war from within and the war from without.

No matter the war cry, who we were could not be taken out of us. It would be unnatural.

No matter the camps we were sent to.

No matter the institutions we were confined in.

No matter how many Bibles were beaten over our heads.

No matter how many chains we were put in.

No matter how many prisons we were locked in.

No matter what. It just simply can not be taken out of us.

Even if we were beaten to death, it went with us.

This was not a sin of choice.

We grew so weary of the battleground so we began to march in a different direction.

We began to celebrate. We started to celebrate who we were. We began our parades, PRIDE PARADE as it was later on named. We celebrated not only as one tribe but we celebrated the differences even within our own tribe.

When we began to celebrate rather than suffer only, we changed as a people. That small voice of shame that haunted us all from within began to fade away. We grew in our unity and were seizing victory.

We became a different people. We were no longer holding our heads down. Our PRIDE was not the pride of the world. It was quite the opposite. Our PRIDE taught us gratitude and humility. It made us a better people. We were more freely able to give.

So, the fight was worth it!

Triangles and rainbows.

Our generation was certainly not the first to suffer. There were many generations before us. Ours was the first to celebrate.

There are two flags my tribe is still waving. One is

our rainbow flag and the other is our black flag with a large pink triangle in the center of it.

The pink triangle flag we wave was given to us by Hitler. This was the color of the triangle placed on all homosexuals in the Nazi camps. Hitler had a color for every type of people there. Ours was pink.

Hitler's triangles were opposite that of the triangle of the Trinity. The triangle of the Trinity of Father, Son and Holy Ghost has its single point at the top of the triangle. Hitler's triangles had its single point at the bottom of the triangle.

So, what do you get when you lay the Trinity triangle over our pink triangle?

The Star of David!

Who says we aren't some of God's chosen one's?

I remember when the conception of this book came to mind and heart, there were only two things I set out to prove. I was going to prove that despite my being gay, I was going to somehow prove my good heart. And that despite my being gay, I was going to prove that I was saved.

In my life, filthy minds voided any good that ever flowed from out of my heart. And the saved part? Well, there was no homosexual that could ever be saved, or so I was told. I knew they were wrong and I was going to prove it. After all, I am a homosexual and I am saved!

The first part, the heart part; well there was not much I could do about that other than to tell my story and continue to live my life and to continue to do good. All I can do is to be an example, to be a little Jesus. If any filthy minds remained, well that was on them and in their hearts.

The second part however, this would be most difficult to prove in and of itself. But too, no matter what I might present, I knew I would not be able to change hearts of stone and minds of steel.

I worked diligently on this second part, not just because of its purpose but because I wanted to be sure in every part of my being that I would not go against the will of God.

Then God said to me one day, "You tell your truth and I will tell My Truth."

For nearly ten years now I have searched and searched and researched all of God's Word. I also bought many different translations of the Bible, trying to be sure I didn't miss anything. God and I had countless conversations on this.

As I was studying one of the newer translations of the Bible, I was reading in the area where the list of sins is written and there it was, the word "homosexual". I turned blood red. Where I came from if you even spoke the word homosexual you were going to hell, but now this!?

The word homosexual was in the Word of God! I feverishly looked up every other passage where the list of sins is written. The word homosexual was everywhere. In one translation the words "sexual immorality" was replaced with the word "homosexual". Now all other sexual sins were no longer listed there. Only the sin of homosexuality. How convenient to now get off scot-free! I know many homosexuals including myself who have no sex at all. I know too, many non-homosexuals whose lives are overrun by their sexual desires. Suddenly, they are no longer on the list.

I remember thinking, "God, what do I do with this?" This brings a whole new battle to the forefront. I was weary as it was!

I knew I could never fight this one. All I could do was to leave this one in God's hands.

When I did this, I saw things in a different light. Finally, I am included in God's Word. I made the cut. I made it on the list.

A sinner saved!

As I chiseled and chiseled and gnawed and gnawed on God's Word some things that I thought were clear became more blurred and things that were blurred became more clear.

But when all is read, said and done, Jesus sets only two commands before us and only two. He said, "You must love the Lord your God with all your heart, all your soul, and all your mind, and all your strength. This is the first and greatest commandment. A second is equally important." You are to "Love your neighbor as yourself."

I am sure glad the word homosexual is not listed here!!

I am even more glad that everything having to do with love is the only thing listed here. And when you think about it, if you truly love yourself then you can't help but to love your neighbor. And when you love God with all that you are, all the rest will naturally follow.

Jesus goes on to add in Matthew 22:40 NLT, "The entire law and all the demands of the prophets are based on these two commandments." If the two laws of love are obeyed then all the other laws will naturally be fulfilled.

Here it was. I had found the key.

God's endless love for us all.

I believe in the end times but I would never dare say how close we are to them. Some days I am sure we are living it out and other days I simply think, God's not even close to gathering up everyone and everything He wants in heaven with Him; the claiming of all for His own.

I believe that for me to even speculate would be like me trying to tell you that I know the hour that Jesus will return.

I only know one thing and that is with each generation that lives we are transformed further and further away from God's perfect creation.

We have fallen far away from Genesis.

Man has departed from woman.

Woman has departed from man.

Husbands have departed from wives.

Wives have departed from husbands.

Fathers have departed from their children.
Children have departed from their fathers.
Mothers have departed from their children.
Children have departed from their mothers.
Brothers have departed from brothers.
Sisters have departed from sisters.
Brothers have departed from sisters.
Sisters have departed from brothers.
Men are no longer men.
Women are no longer women.
Everything has changed.
Even all of creation continues to transform from its original state.
All that was natural back then in that Garden is now unnatural.
There is only one thing that has never changed and that is pride.
Pride will never change.
Nothing is new under the sun.

I saw a robin today. A robin with white wings. Imagine that!

I wonder how many generations it took before this robin's wings that were meant to be black were now the color white.

I know much about our PRIDE. In my tribe we helped each other to live and we helped each other to die. There was no magic formula to it. We just simply helped one another. And we just simply loved each other.

Then the pride of man seeped in. We wanted to be just like the rest of the world. We wanted to blend into all the rest of the world.

The days of our rejoicing dwindled away. We closed up shop and threw away the keys. So much so that we were more alone than ever.

We believed the rest of the world was ready to welcome us. But the world wasn't quite ready for all of that. They were just learning how to tolerate us but for us to blend? They just weren't having it.

We hung in limbo with the solid ground taken out from beneath our feet. We only had ourselves to blame. With this new pride we splintered from each other and our special spot was slipping through our hands.

It was a strange, dark and lonely place to be in. There were no more battle cries. Our unity was gone all in the name of pride. We betrayed each other. We had forsaken our past and all we ever stood up for.

We had no remembrance of our struggles and how we loved one another through them. Our "we" was now becoming one. Each one for themselves.

Now we just were.

Now we were just like all the rest of the world.

I will never forget the massacre in that Orlando nightclub on June 12, 2016. In the Pulse Nightclub, 49 of my people were slaughtered; 53 wounded simply because they were gay. I wept for days!

Hate still lives.
Now I remember!

Hearts have no gender.
Only love or hate.

Romans 12:16 & 18 NLT

16 – Live in harmony with each other. Don't be too proud to enjoy the company of ordinary people. And don't think you know it all!

18 – Do all that you can to live in peace with everyone.

A BRIDE AND THE GROOM

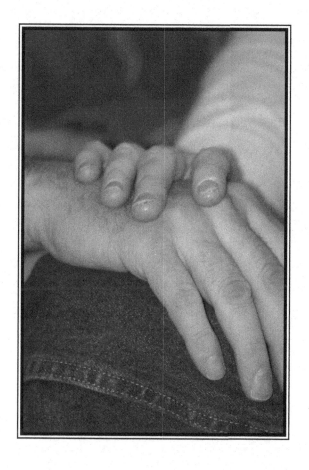

Blessed are those who
are persecuted for
My name's sake...

You may kiss the bride.
Then came baby; or not.

I had survived the pulling down of incest. I was struggling to be loved because of my homosexuality. But there was a greater grief in me that I carried around all these years and that was, I never had that child I so longed for in my latest teens. I guess it was that God given instinct; a maternal instinct given to all women who desire to bear a child.

The desire was deep in me. It became a craving even. A longing in my heart. I weighed carefully where I was in my life and would it be in the best interest of a child. Could I truly raise a child on my own? I could barely care for myself but mostly because of so many of my own wrong choices.

Would I love this child for who he or she might be even as an infant or was I looking for just anyone to love me? Was I this desperate for love? Was it for me and not the child? I knew the latter was most true. And maybe I was just looking for a way to fix all that seemed wrong in me.

Would I be able to give up my addictions; I only had two. I smoked cigarettes and I drank. If I did not give up one or both of these would that baby even make it out of my womb? And if it did would it come out normal? I certainly knew how it felt not to. I also knew that selfishly, for now at least, my addictions would win over what I would need to do.

Then too, to conceive a child would require I be

with a man. Truthfully though this would really not have been too much of a problem. Back then I was sleeping with many men trying to take the gay out of me; so I might "straighten" myself out. But this created yet another problem. Would I know who the father was? I certainly would want to know who the father was if not for the child, for myself.

Then too weighed in the right and wrong in my heart. I knew what the good book said about all this. I knew it was there for my own good but so too man's law told me I should not bear a child except through a husband. This surely would never work considering my condition. I would be deceiving him as well as myself.

I thought long and hard and weighed all these things out in my heart. I believe the ultimate deciding factor for me was that I would have this child mostly for someone to love me. This was not how a mother should be. A mother must love a child more than she loves herself, not the other way around. The expectations and demands that this would have put on an innocent child would have damaged that child for life. And somehow, I knew this.

As God would have it, I never got pregnant. And I made the right decision not to try to become pregnant. Yet despite both of these, the yearning in my heart never stopped.

I carried a grief in me for this child never conceived. A mother's mourning, I guess. I also carried this unborn child with me wherever I went.

My only solace was that I had spared a child. I spared a child from all my wrong reasons to have a child. To have a child for all the wrong reasons. A child spared indeed.

I carried this child imagined in me yet never conceived. The unborn one in my heart.

Sometimes I reflect back and begin to think, what if we could have made it? What if I didn't take matters into my own hands? What if I trusted God enough to bear a child? But then I realized that God was not my worry. I just never trusted myself. There were too many other things heaped upon me. If I weren't yet able to stand where I was, how could I ever train up a child to walk?

A child spared!

My greatest accomplishment.

I would like to think, I imagine even this child of mine that was never conceived is in the arms of God. This child of mine that God never brought the spark of life into, never breathed His breath into, how He is holding this child I have had hidden in my heart for so many years.

This child in the arms of the Groom who will one day come for me.

My life went on. Thank God without that child. The older I got seems the harder life became. It wasn't so much the living that was killing me, it was the wounds that I carried. That thorn and the sword of my incest. I couldn't escape these chains.

I lived as prisoner here on this earth but in some sense, aren't we all? And I know that by the very nature of God's breath each has a purpose here whether born or unborn.

Even that child of mine had a purpose. The mere thought of it made me have to stop and look at my life. I had to evaluate my priorities and make decisions from there.

I had to weigh out my responsibilities and my level of commitment not only to a child but to everything in my life.

I had to look at my spiritual life as well. I was struggling enough knowing the good in me and that according to man, I would never make it to heaven so long as I were a homosexual; that choice thing again.

I knew I was good and I knew I would never get this thorn from out of my side but to add on top of it, to have a child without first being a bride? Well that was going a bit too far. And this was something I did have a choice in.

Mostly, this child of mine taught me the depths of my own heart. It taught me how much I could love, how deep I can love. It taught me of a selfless love. That I chose this child over my own life. This child taught me that my heart was without end.

This child taught me too so much about grief. If I could mourn so over this child I never conceived or even gave birth to then how much more could I grieve over others and things that were all around me?

It was on a very recent Mother's Day when my mother, not meaning any harm, reminded me I was without child. I had been reminded of this time and time again not just by my mother but others as well that "I didn't know what it was like" because I have no children. And every time I was reminded of this a very deep sadness would come over me. Many times, I wanted to say, "Yes I am without child. But no, you will never know the sorrow over sparing a child."

On this day though, I told my mother of my deep yearning to have a child when I was a teenager and of the decision I had made, not to have it and why. My mom never knew this and seemed to see me in a whole new light. In a very tender moment she said to me, "We would have taken it in."

When I got off the phone, I began to weep. I can't tell you the tears I shed that day. They just kept flowing and my heart ached so fiercely. My tears streamed down my face as I moved about that day. I never knew I had so much sorrow in me for the child never conceived in me.

It was on this day that I realized the deep love I was carrying for this child all these days of my life. The love I have always had in my heart.

This child was never conceived in my womb but it was surely conceived in my heart.

In that same conversation my mother then asked,

"Is that why you have always taken young ones in under your wing?" I replied, "I guess so Mom."

Sometimes there is the necessary unseen in order to bring on the appearance of God. To reveal the difference between heaven and earth.

Daniel 4:35 NLT says, "All the people of this earth are nothing compared to Him. He does as He pleases among the angels of heaven and among the people of the earth. No one can stop Him or say to Him, 'What do You mean by doing these things?'"

In so many ways I believe this child in my heart is an unborn angel. An angel never born of this earth. Just maybe that child never conceived is an angel watching over me.

Wouldn't that be just like God!?

I remember as a child looking up to the sky all times of the day. I remember too at night gazing at the heavens looking at all the stars. It seemed as if I had already been there and that this earth was only barrowing me. I certainly longed to go back there. To go back home.

So why couldn't my child have never been barrowed to this earth? Why couldn't God have kept it for His own? Maybe God let me barrow my child if only in my heart.

God created everything including the angels. Maybe, this included my child. Hey, that's it! The one thing I have not done yet is to name my child. I think I will call him or her Angel. I think that will cover everything now.

Maybe this is where I got that added sense in me. Maybe my Angel has been there in that divide between heaven and earth? Maybe Angel has been that seventh sense in me? Maybe Angel has been the one who has been able to discern so well between the light and the dark; the good versus evil. It certainly was not of my own doing. This certainly was from above.

Things have reappeared and vanished from this earth that cannot be explained. I witnessed many of them. None were of this earth. There were never any hands of man that made these things happen.

I know God's eye has always been on me. I know He sees all things but isn't there something too that says He commissions His angels to take charge over us?

Psalm 91:11-12 NLT says, "For He will order His angels to protect you wherever you go. They will hold you up with their hands so you won't even hurt your foot on a stone."

God does see all things but what about His watchers? And what about Heaven's Armies?

God's covenant is real and everlasting. His promise is true. It can never be matched. Not even by the best in all of our humanity.

I know the ring of God's love for me will forever be wrapped around my life. And I know He will be with me where ever I go. We are one.

I know I must live my life and prepare my life every day as if going to that great wedding feast.

There is this parable in Matthew 22 about the wedding feast that was prepared and of those who were first invited, so many refused to come. Then in verses nine and ten it says, "'Now go out to the street corners and invite everyone you see.' So, the servants brought in everyone they could find, good and bad alike, and the banquet hall was filled with guests."

What an invitation. What a promise.

No matter my suffering. No matter my persecution along the way. No matter the hurts I caused others to endure. No matter. I am still welcomed at the wedding feast. And unlike the earthly king who prepared the feast for his son, I will be welcomed in the Kingdom of Heaven by the heavenly Father who is preparing a wedding table for His Son and I where I will be His bride, and He will be my Groom.

I will kiss my Groom.
My Groom will kiss me.

Our heavenly romance will begin.
A romance without end.

My Eternal Love!

Luke 20:34-36 NLT

34 – Jesus replied, "Marriage is for people here on earth.

35 – But in the age to come, those worthy of being raised from the dead will neither marry nor be given in marriage.

36 – And they will never die again. In this respect they will be like angels. They are children of God and children of the resurrection."

JUST A HYMN

Blessed are you who
are mocked because
you are My followers...

I have always had a longing for Jesus.

Just to touch His hem!

His hem was different than any other hymn. His hem was that of healing. The other hymn was a song in my heart.

I needed His hem before I could sing any song.

There is a rhythm in all that is good. There is a melody that plays in the strings of one's heart. The joy in doing good.

I knew I was good. I knew I did good. The good I did was just outside of the framework of what was acceptable by many so my good just seemed not to matter.

I was often mocked and criticized for doing good to those outside my blood tribe. I was so often asked, "Are they saved?" and, "Do they go to church?" and, "What church do they go to?" It was never about any kindness I extended or the goodness that was inside of them. It was always the question, "Are they worthy?"

I stayed so very confused. Weren't we called to love our neighbors? Were our neighbors only limited to those who looked like us, believed like us, thought like us, voted like us? Was everyone else not my neighbor?

I grew not to like this crowd I was hanging with. This click that would not let anyone else in. They were a bunch of stuffed shirts who weren't having any fun at all. None of them ever laughed. Rarely was there a smile on anyone's face.

There clearly was no joy of the Lord in them but boy did they like to sing their hymns.

They didn't seem to know how to laugh or play. That was too ungodly.

Living this way became too much for me. I wanted to cheer. I wanted to rejoice. I needed to laugh. I needed to play at least a little. I had a fun in me that needed to get out.

It certainly felt good to do good. It was wonderful talking to strangers and to hear their stories. This was a whole new world to me. It brought life to me. I loved talking to people who were different than me. The doors of life were swinging open.

This became as an adventure to me. I also found people who were good to me, strangers even.

When all this began with these new found people, I would be asked about my life. In the beginning, I really had nothing much to say at all. My life had been a pretty cookie cutter life. It looked mostly like that of those I had been around all my past years. Inside I was different but that could not be revealed.

I began to ponder this. Why was I not different on the outside? Why was I so boring? Why didn't I have any great stories to tell?

Sure, I could tell people how many hoops I sunk that day or what toys I played on behind the school in that school yard or what new monkey bar tricks I had learned or that I had won at marbles that day or of the new stones I found in the woods behind the tracks or how many balls I caught out in that ball field. But none of these things were any different than any other normal kid.

My insides were different. I just wanted my outside to be as well.

I wasn't sure what I would do if the way things had been would be all that there was to life. I knew I could not bear it. I wasn't meant to live like this.

If I were to venture out some day and find my voice, I certainly wanted to have something more to say.

I wanted to live. I wanted to have stories to tell.

Despite the horrible circumstance of my needing to leave all that I knew, there were also so many blessing that came out of it. I got to start anew.

My life became a story. I saw and experienced so many new things. I had new and different choices. I remember thinking this when I moved to San Francisco. It was a little scary but a good scary. Everything was new and everything was different.

And the people. I never saw such a wonderous blend of people. People of every color and every tribe and from every nation. Where I came from there was only salt and pepper. Mostly salt, only a small dash of pepper.

This new land was rich with culture; every culture, except my Dutch culture back home of course. The variety was wonderful. It was so good to see color of all kinds. Talk about a joyful noise!

It took a little bit but I began to smile. It took me a minute to learn that it was OK to do so.

I fell in love with the freedom. I fell in love with the fact that here, I had no standards to live up to except my own. No one here was comparing me to any other.

Here, I could do good and feel good about it. Here, I could do good and no one would raise an eyebrow. Here, I could do good and it would be welcomed. Here, I could finally breathe.

Here, strangers were kinder.

I found new life here. For the first time in my life I learned what help was. And what it meant to freely give.

I felt I could soar.

And laughter! There was a ton of laughter. We couldn't stop laughing. Oh, what a refreshing breeze. My heart lifted with joy. What had I been missing all my life!?

It was at this time in my life that I would not trade my thorn in for anything. In these days I got a peak at a different side of God.

God was not just black and white. Nor was He the fist pounding God I was raised with.

God was a God of color and variety. God was the creator of color and variety in every sense of the word.

I found out here too that God wants us to enjoy life and live and laugh. He never meant for us to be confined to death here.

I met members of my tribe here. I felt so at home. I was finally home.

Then came the earthquakes. I was only used to tornadoes. These earthquakes; I did not do well with. So, we packed up and headed back to Michigan.

I certainly was not well here. Being back here again. The mood here had not changed. I felt so suffocated especially after being set free. My smile began to fade away. Depression was setting back in. It seemed there was not much here to live for.

Everything was routine. Nothing was exciting. Everything was the same color or so it seemed. Something inside me was dying once again. I knew this feeling. There was little light in it.

Something had to change or I would live a dying life.

So, my partner and I packed up once again and moved to Atlanta, Georgia. We struggled at first but managed to get settled in. It was here our happily ever after came to an end. So much for commitment.

I really believed we would go the long haul. At least I thought we would but Skip; Pat, her formal name, developed other interests.

This was my first real break up. I was not just devastated, I was destroyed. I thought we were different. I believed we were a better people and we just did not do things like this to each other. I not only lost the one I loved; I was also in a state of shock. This couldn't be happening in our tribe. We were going to prove to the world we would not be like them but we would stay together and live up to our commitments.

I wandered around for days, weeks, months even ever so lost and alone. Not only did Skip leave, she took our dog Ben with her. We had been living in this shack-like cabin off the road not far from the shores of Lake Lanier. I was truly all alone and it got very dark at night. I learned to pray a lot here. My heart was sick with pain and it showed.

During this time Skip and I were working together at a marina on the lake. There was this good ole boy who worked there too. He knew I was all alone and, on a few occasions, he would come to visit and check in on me. I think it was his last visit by my choice that he offered me a proposal. No, not like that. He told me he knew people and that he could see to it I would never see Skip again. I knew what he meant.

I hurt. But I didn't hurt that much. Besides, vengeance was not in me; not like that anyway. On that day, I think for the first time in my life I got a clear definition of what Jesus said about being in the world but not of the world.

I needed to move on and find life in me again. I started to go to church. I found out about the MCC church on Highlands Avenue in Atlanta. MCC stands for Metropolitan Community Church. It was known as the "gay church" by outsiders. There are hundreds of them around the world.

The pastor of this particular church was Jimmy

Brock. He was a magnificent preacher. His sermons always sent a message home to me. And I began to sing again. Oh, it was so good to sing again. The songs seemed to have new meaning. This time they included me. This time they were in unison with people just like me. Oh, what a joy.

The congregation was very close. We hung out together a lot. We helped each other in our times of need. We celebrated life, each other and our God. We went on outings and retreats together. We were happy.

I even had a Holy Union in that church. A Holy Union is similar to a marriage commitment only there are no papers involved. It is simply two people committing their lives together before God and the witnesses there. Jimmy Brock performed the ceremony.

Needless to say, that commitment had to end or my life could have been over. Long story. Don't want to go there.

With my tribe, my life has never been boring. Without my tribe, I would have never seen the likes of God, the face of God. I would never have found the One True God.

Did we get everything right? Of course not. Did everyone see the likes of God? I'm sure not? But did I see God through others? Yes, I did.

I grew to know God especially in all the "wrong" places. There grew this deep intimacy between God and I. I had to talk with Him. I had to walk with Him. There was no want in it. I needed Him.

My prayers became not that of kneeling but a moment by moment conversation with God continually. They just had to be. I needed Him too much for it to be any other way.

Do you know of the parable Jesus taught of the ten lepers? All were healed but there was only one who came back rejoicing and thanking Jesus for his healing. Well, I feel like that one leper. My healing is personal but my rejoicing must be heard in the land and to my God.

I will never forget this one Christmas season when I went back home to visit. I went to my sister's church one evening for a Christmas service. I love the old hymns. And they were being sung there that evening. The tears began to well up inside of me then they quietly began to flow down my face. In all the joy of the moment there was a deep sorrow in me.

If they only knew. If they only knew that I am gay. If they knew of me, those church doors that welcomed me in would be the same church doors that would be slammed in my face forever. If they only knew.

Even after all these years, this sorrow was still deep in me. A remembrance of all those church doors slammed in our faces. No wonder our nightclubs became our first churches. At least we were given a stamp of approval there.

There really was a worship in so many of us. We just had nowhere to go with it. It took time, determination and a great desire to understand that we needed no one else's permission to sing praises to God and to worship Him. TO WORSHIP HIM! WITHOUT PERMISSION!

Maybe this is the answer to that pastor's question when he asked me, "Why are there so many of you?" Maybe the answer is, "Because we welcomed anyone inside our doors."

All were welcome at our table.

All are welcome!

Isaiah 45:3 NLT says, "And I will give you treasures hidden in the darkness – secret riches. I will do this so you may know that I am the Lord."

And yes, there is two-stepping in our rejoicing!

I Corinthians 12:6 NKJV– "And there are diversities of activities, but it is the same God who works all in all."

Psalm 150:6 NLT

Let everything that breathes sing praises to the Lord!

Praise the Lord!

THE LAMP POST

Blessed are those who light up the world for they cannot be hidden...

We all are here on equal ground.
All of us are the world. We all are in the world.

God said, "Let there be light." and there was light.
None of us were called to be gate-keepers of the light. Those who won't let the light out into darkness. Those who hold the light all for their own. Those who lurk in the shadows. Those who snuff out even a mere flicker of light.

We all are called to be guardians of the light. We are to see to it that darkness does not overtake the light. We are to see to it that the light radiates over all the earth. We are to extinguish all shadows of darkness and illuminate every glimmer of light. We are to flood this world with the light.

We should see the world through spiritual eyes and not just through the lenses of our earthly eyes.

I lived many years of my life before I understood this in me. I was different in so many other ways that I didn't see this difference in me.

I know if it weren't for my hours upon hours and years upon years of studying God and searching in God's Word, I would have missed this about me.

And I watched God too. I watched Him continually through all His creation. And especially through watching all mankind.

I didn't have hardly any training in my youth but when I was still young, I remember sensing a light and dark in areas as I was passing through them.

It was in San Francisco where I began to pay more attention to the flickers of light and the flecks of dark.

When I moved to Atlanta this sensing became even greater. I could ride through a neighborhood and I could tell right away whether there was more light there or whether there was more dark there. Whether my spirit was welcomed or whether my spirit would be hastened away. It was like a discerning of spirits.

At first this seemed to kind of spook me. But as time went on, I began to use this to help me figure out where I was to go.

I moved around a lot in Georgia. I mean a lot. I lived on every side of Atlanta, except the south side. And I lived many places in the heart of Atlanta.

I began to use this foresight to determine what neighborhoods I would move into. Was my spirit at rest there?

No one knew this was going on inside of me. I might have been locked up if they did.

I began to pay even closer attention to this spirit thing in me. I started to bring it indoors. How was my spirit under the roof that was over my head? Was it at peace or was there a bit of a tug-of-war going on?

Many times, by the time I paid that close enough of attention, it was too late. I was already in the door. And most of the time someone was in there with me.

Maybe this was where I began to then pay ever so close attention to people. How did each one affect my spirit? What was my spirit doing? How was my spirit doing?

Was it restless or welcomed?

This one scared me. It's one thing to pass by a neighborhood and be free to keep going. But this people thing? This could be right under my roof.

My involvement with people eventually began to change. It was like my spirit became my own personal watchdog.

Ever so slowly, I began to sit at a distance with people, spiritually I mean. I seemed no longer to be rushing in.

Then I began to weigh in on my words and in on their every word too. After all, there is a spirit in each one of us.

I became keen in all things. Idle chatter no longer had any value in my life. I just had no time or energy for it.

I had always seemed to like to be alone even as a kid but being raised in a household with eight others there was barely any time to decide if I liked being alone more than not. Being around people became more of a habit, a norm even.

So, normally and habitually most of the time I was around people. But with this spirit discovery in me I began to rethink my fondness for being alone.

Being around people was beginning to be exhausting. Not that the conversation wore me out, it was the weighing of the words. People were telling more about themselves than they were even aware of.

I'm sure they would have shut their mouths if they only knew. But to them it was casual conversation.

This too wore me out.

I grew to love only rich exchanges.

I would come to life if words were said that would ignite me. Or words I might say that would bring life to someone else. I could talk all night if there was this kind of sharing. I loved to learn from others. I loved their stories. I loved the realness of life in these kinds of words.

Having someone close like this was very, very rare. Almost not at all. So, I grew to love my being alone more. I called it my recharge. I got pretty good at it.

I did have much fun in life. My life was filled with fun.

The church outings like the monk monastery.

The activities with the Women's Outdoor Network where we went white-water rafting, mountain biking, hiking and camping.

The times I went horse-back riding.

All the sports events I organized.

I had my own pick up basket-ball crowd at that local gym. Out of it came my own basket-ball team.

I organized my own softball team.

I organized touch-football on Sunday mornings in Piedmont Park.

And all those years going to the Women's Final Four.

I trained for the 5k PRIDE run. As well as worked out on my own for hours each week.

I went to baseball games and football games. The Atlanta Braves and the Atlanta Falcons. I had season tickets even for one year of the Falcons.

I got to be a part of the 1996 Olympics when they came to Atlanta. Who can say that?

And I can never forget all the dancing. Those nights two-stepping. What fun! My people loved to dance.

I really did have many great things in my life. I have had things in my life that others can only dream of.

Yet through all of this, being alone was where I wanted to be increasingly more and more. I found my peace there.

God kept whispering it so.

One of the most telling times was when some of my best friends and I went downtown one evening to enjoy the 1996 Olympic festivities. It was a hot sunny evening. I think there was about six or seven of us. We were having a good time and shopping at all the vendor booths. The streets were packed. I turned my head but for an instant and when I looked back, everyone I had been with had vanished; literally vanished. Not a single one I had come with could be found. I looked briefly but when I could not find a one, I knew I would stay all alone.

I should have been panicked but surprisingly I was very calm despite the massive crowd, despite me being all alone; briefly wondering how I would get home.

We were in the heart of downtown Atlanta and my

place was just on the outskirts across from Piedmont Park. I can't even remember how we got downtown or how being all alone, I made it home. I only knew I was not afraid and that I was somewhat glad to be going home where I could be all alone. Everyone had met at my place so I just peaceably waited on the balcony till they all came back. They were still all together. I remember thinking how lucky I was to have been able to quietly sit on my balcony and be alone on that warm summer night.

Another place God made it very clear to me that He wanted me all for His own was in that nightclub, The Other Side. Yes, this truly was the name of that place. This was the same place where a bomb went off that Saturday night during the Olympics. As God would have it, I was not there that night.

I was a regular at The Other Side. This was not your neighborhood bar. This was a nightclub. The dance floor was bigger than my entire apartment. Anyway, this is how regular I was. I would walk in the door and I would have to pass that dance floor before I reached the bar. Well, before I could get to the bar the bartender, Jules would have an open beer waiting for me on the corner of that bar.

This place that I played in was a great testing ground for me. I learned so much of myself there and of other people.

One of my first and biggest tests was that of faithfulness to myself.

I had literally escaped from this over eight-year relationship. My partner was the one who I had the Holy Union with. Right after the Holy Union my partner grew very abusive. So much so that after I escaped, I was stalked by her for three years after.

I was so angry and frustrated by this failure not only by the two of us, but also within our community. We were proving to the rest of the world that we were no different than them. We were proving that we too could not live up to our commitments to live out a lasting relationship. I just did not understand it. Nearly everyone I knew, their greatest pursuit in life was to find that "Till death do us part." relationship.

But mostly, I was so very angry that despite all my monogamy in my two "lasting" relationships, both had failed. My commitment nor my monogamy seemed to matter at all.

This time, this time though I was going to live free to be; no commitments. I would sleep with whoever I desired to be with. I was determined to try this part in me just to see if it was truly in me. My heart and my love obviously carried no value at all. I decided my priorities needed to change.

Well, I sat on that bar stool night after night trying to make myself interested in someone. Some were interested in me. Seems though I had a "Do Not Disturb" sign hanging around my neck.

I wasn't the pursuing type. Nor did I really like being pursued. I was in quite a dilemma. But this dilemma was not my problem. My problem became very clear to me. I could not lay down with anyone unless I loved them and they loved me and that we were equally committed to each other. Still I knew in my heart that I would not ever attempt such a thing again.

The other thing that happened to me there was the other people. It was no longer the watching of them, it became the observing of them. Before I watched them more for entertainment but now, I was observing their faces. I was seeing a deeper in them. A darker in them. It wasn't that they were dark but inside there was a darkness. An empty hole darkness. A sadness. A longing. It was like looking in a mirror.

It's easy to put on a happy face when you're out and about. But I could see the sad face in each one of them. I either knew them or knew of so many of the people there. But I was seeing them all so differently now. And I saw the same thing in the strangers there as well.

It wasn't long after that I just had to quit going there. The dancing lost its play and the people were too much of a reminder of what was inside of me.

So alone became my favorite place to be.

Eventually, I moved to Douglasville, Georgia; some twenty minutes west of Atlanta. Be careful what you wish for. I was entirely alone. So many of my friends had moved away. The community was falling apart. All of our support systems, organizations and even our bars had shut down or were in the process of closing. Even our church had split in two. We were scattered everywhere. Everything we worked so hard for, all the good we did was gone and forgotten.

So, yes, I was absolutely all alone.

Except there was One.

I was sitting there, staring God in the face.

There was no other place to go.

Jeremiah 29:13 NLT had never more true to me, "If you look for Me wholeheartedly, you will find Me."

This little light of mine!

Let it shine.

Let it shine.

"The Lord bless you and keep you;
The Lord make His face shine upon you,
And be gracious to you;
The Lord lift up His countenance upon you,
And give you peace."

Numbers 6:24-26 NKJV

John 1:3-5 NLT

3 — God created everything through Him, and nothing was created except through Him.

4 — The Word gave life to everything that was created, and His life brought light to everyone.

5 — The light shines in the darkness, and the darkness can never extinguish it.

ABOUT THE AUTHOR

I currently live in Grand Rapids, Michigan.

I began writing over ten years ago. My writings began when I developed a sense of urgency to address childhood incest and to express the lasting effects it had in my own life so I wrote, "Splinters from my Rocking Chair – A Journey Through Incest Survival".

After awakening this deep, dark part of my life, I then also became very aware of all the splendors in my life. This led me to write, "Whispers from my Rocking Chair – The Transformation of an Incest Survivor".

Before I could finish the book "Whispers", a seed was planted in me to write yet another book. This book, "Imaginary Heart" was conceived in me.

It has taken me many years and a great wrestling with God to understand His calling on me to complete this book. All the answers came to me when one day God simply said to me, "You tell your truth and I will tell My Truth." Everything flowed from then on out.

One of my favorite hobbies is photography. I am grateful for the opportunity to share just some of my photos in the creative design of the covers and interiors of my three books; His three books.

In moving forward, I believe that God is not done with me and that I need to write yet again. This time it will be about the wonderment of all God has created and of all things seen.

Printed in the United States
By Bookmasters

Printed in the United States
By Bookmasters